The Encyclopedia of Junior Science

Volume 4

Cheryl Jakab   *David Keystone*

CHELSEA CLUBHOUSE

An Imprint of Chelsea House Publishers

This edition published in 2009 in the United States of America by Chelsea Clubhouse, an imprint of Chelsea House Publishers.

First published in 2007 by
MACMILLAN EDUCATION AUSTRALIA PTY LTD
15–19 Claremont Street, South Yarra 3141

Chelsea Clubhouse
An imprint of Chelsea House Publishers
132 West 31st Street
New York, NY 10001

Chelsea Clubhouse books are available at special discounts when purchased in bulk quantities for businesses, associations, institutions, or sales promotions. Please call our Special Sales Department in New York at (212) 967-8800 or (800) 322-8755.

You can find Chelsea House on the World Wide Web at http://www.chelseahouse.com

Library of Congress Cataloging-in-Publication Data

Jakab, Cheryl.
  The encyclopedia of junior science / Cheryl Jakab, David Keystone. — 1st ed.
  p. cm.
  Includes index.
  ISBN-13: 978-1-60413-554-1
  ISBN-10: 1-60413-554-9
  1. Science—Encyclopedias, Juvenile. I. Keystone, David. II. Title.

  Q121.J35 2009
  503—dc22

                                        2008038113

Edited by Miriana Dasovic, Georgina Garner, and Ruth Jelley
Text and cover design by Christine Deering
Page layout by Raul Diche
Photo research by Legend Images
Scientific and technical illustrations by Alan Laver
Earth, environment, plant, and nature cycles illustrations by Richard Morden
Life cycles, people, and miscellaneous illustrations by Ben Spiby
Plant and animal body systems illustrations by Guy Holt
Human full-body systems illustrations by Jeff Lang
Space illustrations by Melissa Webb
Maps courtesy of Geo Atlas

Printed in the United States of America

Acknowledgements
The author and the publisher are grateful to the following for permission to reproduce copyright material:

Front cover photographs: wind turbine, courtesy of Photos.com; amethyst © Dusipuffi/Dreamstime.com; hot air balloon, courtesy of Digital Vision; green frog © Pufferfishy/Dreamstime.com; Great Ocean Road coastline, Victoria, Australia, courtesy of Jiri Lochman/Lochman Transparencies; rocket launch, courtesy of Photodisc.

Photos supplied courtesy of: TSADO/NASA/Tom Stack/Auscape, p. 47; BrandX Pictures, p. 39 (dragonfly, grasshopper, butterfly, bug, beetle, bee); © Patrice Latron/Corbis, p. 17 (top); © Crni_arapin/Dreamstime.com, p. 26 (top right); © Dreamphoto1000/Dreamstime.com, p. 42 (right); © Gizmo/Dreamstime.com, p. 17 (bottom); © Matthewt/Dreamstime.com, p. 48 (top); © Shahinkia/Dreamstime.com, p. 21 (right); Coo-ee Historical Picture Library, p. 11 (bottom); Coo-ee Picture Library, p. 9 (center); Corbis Digital Stock, pp. 11 (top), 25; Digital Vision, p. 42 (left); Gordon Flynn, pp. 23 (right), 35, 45 (top); Calvin J. Hamilton, p. 46 (bottom); © creacart/iStockphoto, p. 43 (worm); © Patrick Roherty/iStockphoto, p. 9 (right); © Jupiterimages Corporation, p. 36; Dennis Sarson/Lochman Transparencies, p. 18 (top); Photographer G. R. 'Dick' Roberts © Natural Sciences Image Library, pp. 26 (top left), 44; © Peter E. Smith, Natural Sciences Image Library, p. 19 (top); Photodisc, pp. 16 (bottom), 24 (bottom right), 31 (right), 38 (top), 39 (fly); PhotoEssentials, pp. 29 (left), 46 (top); Photolibrary, p. 18 (bottom left); Photolibrary/Science Photo Library, pp. 8 (bottom), 27 (top); Photolibrary/Eye Of Science/Science Photo Library, p. 18 (bottom right); Photolibrary/Vaughan Fleming/Science Photo Library, p. 9 (left); Photolibrary/James King-Holmes/Science Photo Library, p. 15; Photolibrary/Mike McNamee/Science Photo Library, p. 26 (bottom); Photolibrary/Allan Morton/Dennis Milon/Science Photo Library, p. 5; Photolibrary/Sheila Terry/Science Photo Library, p. 40 (top); Photos.com, p. 7, 12, 14, 24 (left & top right), 29 (right), 30 (top & center), 33 (bottom), 43 (all except worm).

While every care has been taken to trace and acknowledge copyright, the publisher tenders their apologies for any accidental infringement where copyright has proved untraceable. Where the attempt has been unsuccessful, the publisher welcomes information that would redress the situation.

Introduction

The Encyclopedia of Junior Science introduces the "big ideas in science" to students using simple scientific language. The "big ideas" introduce key science concepts, build knowledge and understanding, and demonstrate these at work in everyday examples.

The encyclopedia contains approximately 270 entries relating to one of six different branches of science:

- Biology
- Chemistry
- Earth
- Environment
- Physics
- Space

How to Use the Encyclopedia

The entries in *The Encyclopedia of Junior Science* are arranged alphabetically. There are several ways to find an entry or to find information on a topic, using Volumes 1 to 9 and Volume 10, the index volume.

Guide Letter
Use the guide letter at the top of the right-hand page to locate an entry that begins with that letter. You can flip the pages to find where a new letter begins.

Guide Words
Use the guide word or words under the guide letter to find the entry you are looking for. The first guide word is the first entry and the second guide word is the last entry on the double-page spread.

Branch of Science
The tab at the top of the page indicates the branch of science to which the entry relates. Sometimes entries relate to more than one branch of science.

Introductory Definition
Read the first paragraph for a general definition and simple information about the entry. Read on for more information on the topic.

Index Volume
You can also use the alphabetical or thematic indexes in Volume 10 to find an entry or other related information. If you are looking for a famous scientist, you will find a complete list of scientists that appear in the encyclopedia in the index volume.

The index volume also contains useful tables, charts, classifications, and scales relating to specific areas of science.

See Also
Use the *See Also* cross-references to find more information on the entry, and to find other related information.

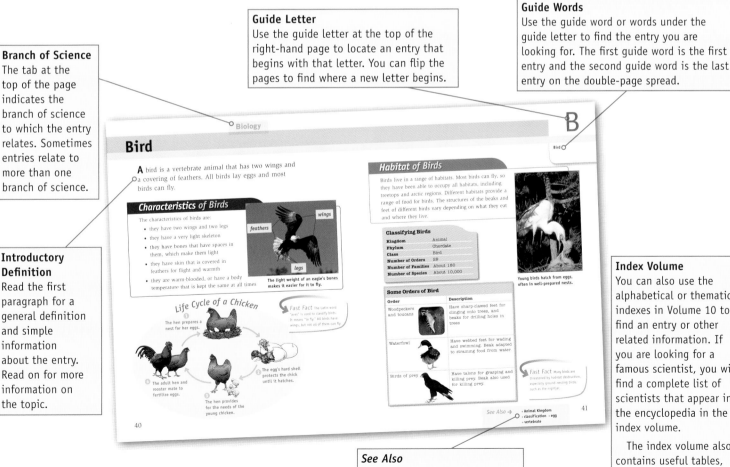

Galaxy

A galaxy is a group of billions of stars in space. Galaxies also contain dust, gas, planets, moons, and other space objects. Galaxies are held together by gravity. Earth is in a galaxy called the Milky Way.

Shapes of Galaxies

Galaxies are classified according to their shape. Galaxies can be classified as spiral, elliptical, barred spiral, or irregular.

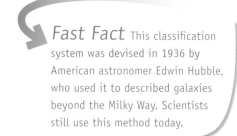

Fast Fact This classification system was devised in 1936 by American astronomer Edwin Hubble, who used it to described galaxies beyond the Milky Way. Scientists still use this method today.

A spiral galaxy has a flattened disk shape with a bulge in the center and long, curved arms.

An elliptical galaxy can be a round or flattened egg shape.

A barred spiral galaxy is a spiral galaxy with a bar-shaped center.

An irregular galaxy has no set shape.

Structure of Galaxies

Galaxies are made up of many stars. There may be hundreds of millions or even billions of stars in a galaxy. Galaxies contain other objects too, such as dust, gas, planets, moons, and comets.

Galaxies vary in size from a few thousand light-years across to more than half a million light-years across. They give out (emit) many types of energy, including gamma rays, radio waves, visible light, and X-rays.

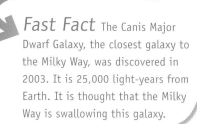

Fast Fact The Canis Major Dwarf Galaxy, the closest galaxy to the Milky Way, was discovered in 2003. It is 25,000 light-years from Earth. It is thought that the Milky Way is swallowing this galaxy.

Beyond the Milky Way

Only three galaxies beyond the Milky Way can be seen from Earth without a telescope: the Large Magellanic Cloud, the Small Magellanic Cloud, and the Andromeda Galaxy.

These three galaxies can be seen with the naked eye on clear, dark nights. They appear as small, hazy patches of light.

Every star seen in the night sky is a part of the Milky Way Galaxy.

Visible Galaxies Beyond the Milky Way	
Galaxy	Distance from Earth
Large Magellanic Cloud	179,000 light-years
Small Magellanic Cloud	210,000 light-years
Andromeda Galaxy	2,900,000 light-years

See Also → •gravity •light-year •ray •universe •waves

Gas

A gas is a substance with no set structure. Gases fill any space they occupy. A gas consists of molecules that move about freely. Gas is one of the three common states of matter.

Properties of Gases

Fast Fact Some gases, such as carbon monoxide, are poisonous to humans and other living things.

The properties of gases are:

- they have the lowest density of all forms of matter
- they expand in every direction
- they may have color and odor
- they can be compressed, or pressed into a small space
- they mix readily with other gases
- they may react with some gases, liquids, or solids

Structure of Gases

Gases do not have a set structure. The molecules of a gas bounce away from each other, so that the gas spreads out. The molecules are widely spaced and can move freely in any direction. A gas, such as air, can be a mixture of different elements, or it can contain just one element, such as oxygen.

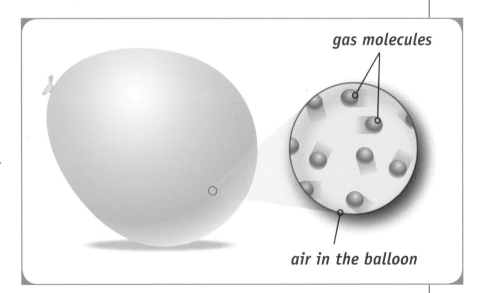

gas molecules

air in the balloon

The air in the balloon spreads out to fill the space it is enclosed in.

Common Gases

Some common gases include hydrogen, oxygen, carbon dioxide, nitrogen, and methane gases.

Examples of Gases

Gas	chemical symbol	Color and Odor	Volume of Earth's Atmosphere	Found In
Oxygen	O_2	None	21%	Water, rocks, living things, air
Nitrogen	N_2	None	78%	Minerals, all living matter, sea, air
Carbon Dioxide	CO_2	None	0.04%	Plants (taken in to make food), animals (breathed out into air)

Uses of Gases

Gases are used in many ways. Methane is used as a fuel for heating and cooking in the home.

Compressed gases can be used to lift or expand things, such as a bicycle pump squeezing air into a small space to inflate a tire.

Gases that expand when heated can transfer heat and cause an object to lift. In a hot-air balloon, a burner heats air particles, which then spread out to fill the balloon and make it light enough to rise.

Fast Fact Dry ice is a very cold, solid form of carbon dioxide that is used in theater performances to create fog or mist.

Methane, commonly called natural gas, is the gas used for cooking on a stove.

See Also → • air • atmosphere • liquid • matter • physical property • solid

Gear

A gear is a wheel that turns another wheel. Gearwheels have cogs that connect them with other wheels. Gears change the effort needed to do work. Gears are used in machines to make work easier.

How Gears Work

Gears work by transferring effort to other wheels. Gearwheels have cogs, or teeth, that connect them to other wheels. When one gearwheel is turned, the other wheel turns in the opposite direction. If the wheels are different sizes, the smaller of the wheels will turn faster than the larger wheel.

Turning the large wheel makes the little wheel turn faster.

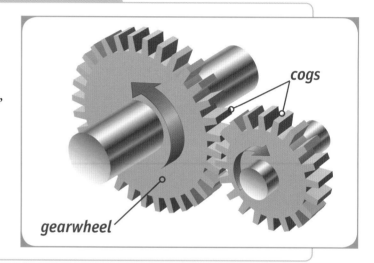

cogs

gearwheel

This modern bicycle has gearwheels of various sizes that are all smaller than the two wheels it runs on.

Fast Fact The first bicycles had no pedals or gears, and were ridden by people pushing their feet against the ground.

See Also → • force • machine
• wheel and axle

Gemstone

A gemstone is a rare stone valued for its beauty. Most gemstones are found as crystals in rocks.

Properties of Gemstones

The properties of gemstones depend on the minerals in them. The properties of gemstones are:

- they have a varying luster, or shine
- they vary in color and transparency, or the amount of light that can pass through them
- they have a crystal form, or geometric shape
- they have different levels of hardness
- they have different types of markings

Types of Gemstones

Gemstones that come from rocks are called mineral gemstones. They include jade, ruby, emerald, and opal. Pearl and coral are also gemstones, but they are formed by living things. Pearls form in oysters, and coral forms from coral animals.

Fast Fact Cutting and polishing gemstones reveals their beauty.

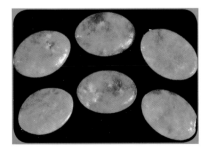

Jade is a polished gemstone of jadeite, which is found in metamorphic rock.

Opal forms in sedimentary rock.

Coral forms from the skeletons of tiny sea animals.

Pearl forms in the shell of living oysters.

See Also → • coral • crystal
• diamond • mineral
• physical property • rock

9

Gene

A gene is a section of chromosome that contains a set of coded instructions. The combined effect of genes determines the characteristics of a living organism.

Structure of Genes

Genes are small sections of the **d**eoxyribo**n**ucleic **a**cid (**DNA**) molecules that are found in a chromosome. Each gene is made up of several thousand base pairs, or "rungs," of DNA.

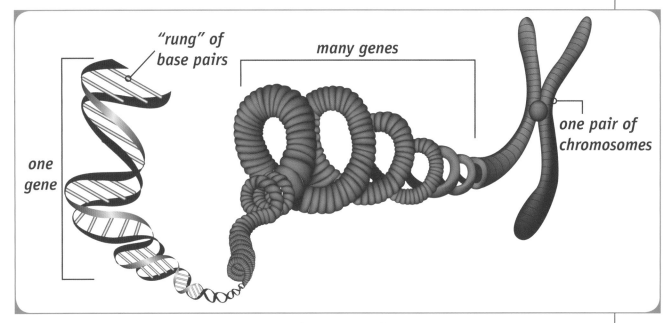

"rung" of base pairs

many genes

one gene

one pair of chromosomes

Thousands of gene sections make up the very long DNA molecule in a chromosome.

Function of Genes

Genes control how cells grow and how they work. In every pair of human chromosomes, one chromosome comes from the mother and one from the father. In a full set of 23 paired chromosomes, there are about 30,000 genes. The combination of these different genes controls which characteristics will be passed on to, or inherited by, the young.

Fast Fact DNA is short for deoxyribonucleic acid, which is the chemical that genes are made from.

Genetics

Genetics is the scientific study of genes and inheritance. The study of genetics explores how characteristics are passed on from parents to children through genetic material. Geneticists are scientists who study genes and their effects.

> *Fast Fact* Human DNA is very similar to the DNA of chimpanzees. The chimpanzee is considered the closest living relative of humans.

Parents may pass on their characteristics, such as hair color, to their children through genes.

Developments in Genetics

1860s	1900	1953
Austrian scientist and monk Gregor Mendel conducts experiments by breeding pea plants, but his work is overlooked.	Plant breeders, or botanists, and other scientists rediscover the work of Mendel.	James Watson and Francis Crick work out a structure for DNA, showing how genetic inheritance could work.

Gregor Mendel

See Also → • chromosomes
• inheritance

Geological Time

Geological time is a timescale of the history of the Earth as shown by its rocks. The timescale begins with the formation of the Earth about 4,600 million years ago and comes up to today. Geological time is divided into eras and periods.

Geological Evidence

The geological timescale is based on several types of evidence:

- the layering of rock in the Earth's crust, which gives a compared, or relative, age

- the fossils within the rocks, which indicate a relative age

- the radioactivity in some rocks, which can be used to give an actual age in years

Upper layers of rock were deposited after the layers of rock below them.

The Relative Age of Rock Layers

The relative age of rock layers is based on the idea that lower layers of rock are older than the layers on top. This method of relative dating is called stratigraphy. This method does not measure age or time in years, but indicates which layers, or strata, are younger or older than others.

The Actual Age of Rock Layers

The actual age of rock layers can be found using radiometric dating techniques. These techniques measure the natural radioactivity in rock and use its rate of decay over time to judge the age of the rock. Radioactive materials have been used to calculate the actual age of rocks and other materials since the early 1900s.

Earth's Geological Timescale

Earth's geological timescale is divided into eras. The Cenozoic era is the most recent era. Eras are further divided into periods, such as the Ediacaran period. The eras and periods are classified mainly according to the once-living things found in the rocks. This is because different species of plants and animals evolved on Earth during particular periods.

Fast Fact The Ediacaran period (600–542 million years ago) was added to the timescale in 1994. It is named after the Ediacara Range, in South Australia, where fossils from this period were first identified.

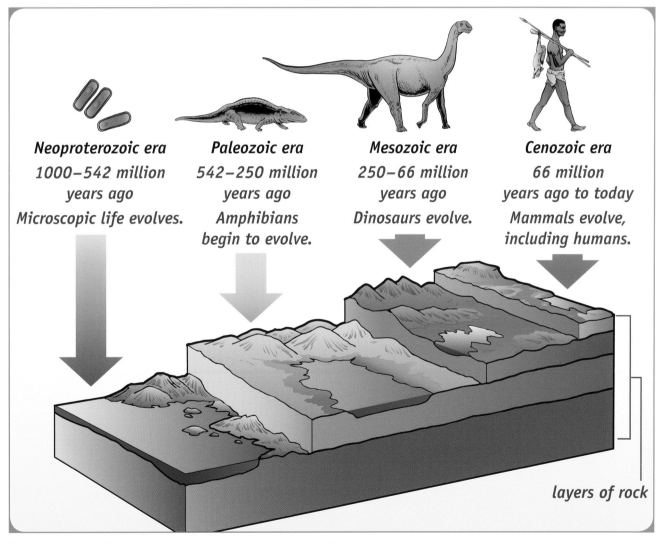

Neoproterozoic era
1000–542 million years ago
Microscopic life evolves.

Paleozoic era
542–250 million years ago
Amphibians begin to evolve.

Mesozoic era
250–66 million years ago
Dinosaurs evolve.

Cenozoic era
66 million years ago to today
Mammals evolve, including humans.

layers of rock

The geological timescale suggests what Earth was like during the period when each layer of rock was laid down.

See Also → • evolution • fossil • geology • radioactivity

Geology

Geology is the study of the Earth's crust. This includes the crust's movements, and its materials and landforms, such as rocks, soils, rivers, oceans, mountains, caves, and glaciers. Geologists are scientists who study Earth's materials.

Key ideas in geology

The key ideas in geology are:

- The Earth's crust is cracked into plates that are constantly moving.

- Most rock is formed in layers. The oldest layers of rock are generally found at the bottom of a rock formation, and the youngest rock is found at the top.

- Rocks from different places that contain the same types of fossils are generally the same age.

- Ice ages are times in the Earth's history when parts of the Earth froze over.

Fast Fact The word "geology" comes from the Greek words "geo," meaning "earth," and "logy," meaning "discussion."

The geological features of an area include landforms, such as rivers and streams.

Branches of Geology

There are many branches of geology. Each branch specializes in some aspect of Earth's materials and landforms.

Branches of Geology

Branch	Focus
Geomorphology	Earth's surface and changes that occur to it
Geophysics	Earth's interior, magnetic properties, and earthquakes
Glacial geology	The formation and effects of glaciers
Hydrology	The movement and spread of Earth's waters
Mineralogy	The characteristics and formation of minerals
Oceanography	Ocean characteristics, such as currents, and their effects
Paleontology	The formation, age, and classification of fossils
Petrology	Igneous, metamorphic, and sedimentary rocks
Planetology	The chemical and physical properties of planets
Volcanology	Volcanoes and the processes that cause them

Geologists

Geologists study many aspects of the Earth and its minerals, including resources such as oil and coal.

Geologists called seismologists study the shock waves that travel through the Earth's crust.

Fast Fact Rocks and soil samples collected during the *Apollo* space missions to the Moon in 1969–1972 are similar to rocks found on Earth.

A seismometer is used by seismologists to collect information about the types of rocks and the different layers in Earth's crust.

See Also → • Earth • geological time
• ice age
• plates of the Earth

Glacier

A glacier is a large mass of ice that moves slowly across land. Glaciers form where large amounts of ice build up and move downhill due to the force of gravity.

How a Glacier Forms

Snow builds up on high mountains and forms ice.

The moving ice forms a river of ice, called a glacier.

Gravity forces the ice to move slowly down the mountainside.

Types of Glaciers

There are two main types of glaciers:

- Valley glaciers are long, narrow bodies of ice that fill high mountain valleys. They are found in the Andes of South America, the European Alps, and the Southern Alps of New Zealand.

- Continental glaciers are broad, thick sheets of ice sloping downwards to the sea. They are found in Antarctica and Greenland.

Fast Fact Today most glaciers are melting and getting smaller, possibly because of increasing temperatures on Earth.

A glacier can carve a U-shaped valley in the land.

16

See Also → • erosion • ice age • weathering

Glass

Glass is a hard, brittle, transparent substance. It is made by heating a mixture of silica, or sand, and other ingredients.

How Glass is Made

Glass is made in stages.

1 A mixture of ingredients such as silica, sodium carbonate (soda ash), and calcium carbonate (limestone) is heated to around 2,732 degrees Fahrenheit (1,500 degrees Celsius). This forms molten glass, which is a liquid.

2 Molten glass can be put in molds or blown into shape.

3 The shaped glass is cooled slowly, to prevent shattering.

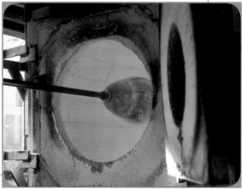

Molten glass is formed in an oven called a kiln.

Properties of Glass

The properties of glass are:

• it is brittle and easily shattered

• when melted, it is malleable, or easy to shape

• it becomes transparent when cooled

Fast Fact When glass is recycled, it is reheated, remelted, and shaped into new glass.

Uses of Glass

Different types of glass are used for different purposes:

• Heatproof glass is used in oven doors.

• Shatterproof glass is used in vehicle windshields.

• Thin, flexible tubes of glass in the form of optic fibers are used in communications systems.

Strong, shatterproof glass is used in windshields.

See Also → • **physical property**
• **quartz** • **sand** • **solid**

17

Gold

chemical symbol **Au**

Gold is a precious metal. It is yellow in color and soft. It does not corrode or tarnish easily. Gold is an element.

Properties of Gold

The properties of gold are:

- it is a soft metal and is yellow in color
- it is highly malleable, or easy to shape
- it resists corrosion, or breaking down by other chemicals
- it forms alloys with other metals
- it is ductile, meaning that it can be stretched and drawn out into wire
- it conducts electricity and heat.

Small lumps of gold are called nuggets.

Uses of Gold

Gold is useful because it does not tarnish easily. It is used to make jewelry and coins. It is used in electronics and in measuring instruments. Gold can be alloyed, or combined with, copper or silver.

Fast Fact Gold occurs in veins, or cracks, in rocks. It can also be found in the form of grains and nuggets in streams.

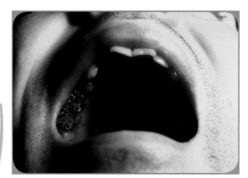

Gold can be alloyed with silver or platinum to make tooth fillings.

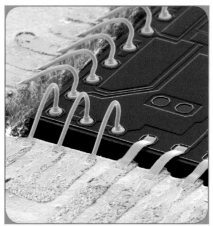

The connecting wires on a computer chip are often made of gold.

See Also → • alloy • metal • mineral • physical property

Grass

A grass is a flowering plant with long, thin leaves. There are about 9,000 species of grass. Some grasses are only a few inches tall. Others, such as bamboo, grow to over 130 feet (40 meters) tall.

Structure of Grasses

A grass plant has a stem, sheaths and blades that make up the leaves, and roots. The stem can be hollow, soft, or woody. The roots are usually fibrous, or stringy.

Flowers grow at the end of the grass stem.

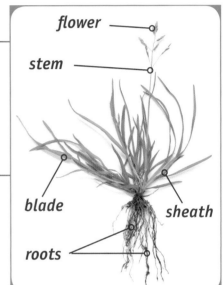

flower

stem

blade

sheath

roots

Fast Fact Most of the world's cereal crops come from just four grasses: wheat, barley, maize, and rice.

Life Cycle of Wheat

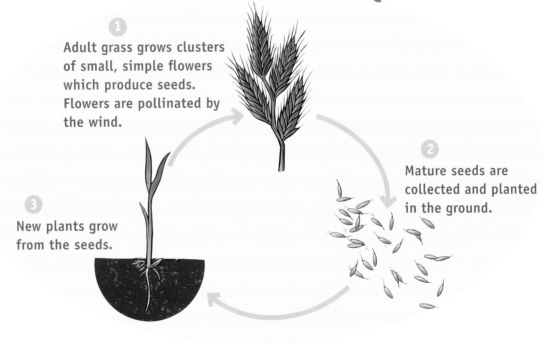

1 Adult grass grows clusters of small, simple flowers which produce seeds. Flowers are pollinated by the wind.

2 Mature seeds are collected and planted in the ground.

3 New plants grow from the seeds.

See Also → • botany • flower
• Plant Kingdom
• pollination

19

Gravity

Gravity is a force that attracts, or pulls. Every piece of matter in the universe pulls on every other piece of matter.

How Gravity Works

The strength of the pull of gravity depends on the mass of both objects and the distance between them. Objects with greater mass have stronger gravitational pulls. On Earth, gravity pulls objects toward the center of the Earth. This makes things fall to the ground when they are dropped.

The closer two objects are to each other, the stronger the pull of gravity between them. The Earth's pull on an object sitting on the surface of the Earth is stronger than the Earth's pull on the same object if it was sitting on the Moon.

Gravity gives an object weight. An object on Earth is pulled downward with stronger force than an object would be pulled to the Moon, which is smaller than the Earth and has a weaker pull. This means the object would weigh less on the Moon.

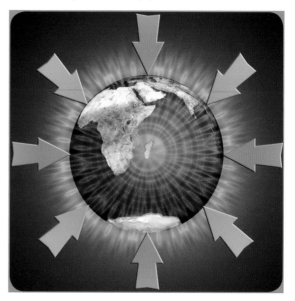

Earth's gravity pulls matter toward its center.

G-force

The Italian physicist Galileo Galilei (1564–1642) experimented with gravitational force, or g-force. He dropped objects with different weights, such as a nail and a hammer, from the same height and found that they landed at the same time. This is because g-force pulls all objects at the same rate, regardless of their weight.

Fast Fact English physicist Isaac Newton suggested that the planets were pulled around the Sun by gravity in the same way that a falling apple was pulled to Earth.

The Importance of Gravity

- In space, gravity is the force that holds the Solar System together. It keeps planets orbiting around the Sun, and keeps moons orbiting around the planets.

- Gravity stops all things on Earth, such as the atmosphere, oceans, and living creatures, from drifting off into space.

- Gravity is weak compared to other forces. You can pick up an object that is more massive than your arms, because your muscles can overcome the weak force of gravity.

Resisting Gravity

Parachutes and gliders use air resistance to work against the pull of gravity and slow their fall. Their shapes control how much air is caught.

Our muscles can overcome the pull of gravity.

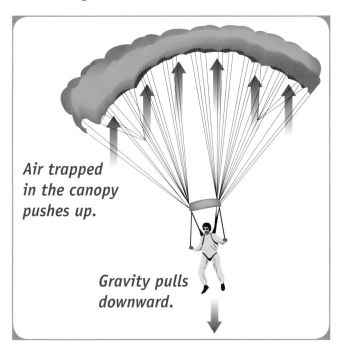

Air trapped in the canopy pushes up.

Gravity pulls downward.

The air caught in the parachute canopy slows down the parachutist's fall.

Fast Fact When objects on Earth fall, they fall at a speed that increases by 32.1 feet (9.8 meters) per second.

See Also → • acceleration • black hole • center of gravity • force • star • weight

Greenhouse Effect

The greenhouse effect is the trapping of the Sun's heat in Earth's atmosphere. This helps make the planet suitable for life. Pollution in the atmosphere is increasing the greenhouse effect.

How the Greenhouse Effect Works

Greenhouse gases in the atmosphere act like a sheet of glass on a greenhouse, trapping some of the heat that comes from the Sun. The atmosphere created by the greenhouse gases stops most of the heat escaping back into space. The trapped heat keeps the planet warm enough to support life.

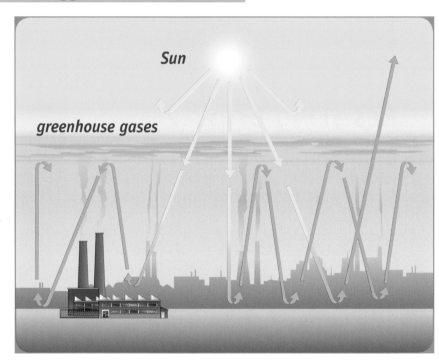

The natural greenhouse effect, which keeps the Earth warm, is increased by human activity.

Increased Greenhouse Effect

When too many gases such as carbon dioxide are released into the atmosphere, they trap too much heat. This causes temperatures across the planet to increase. This increase in temperature is known as global warming. Global warming is caused by human activities, such as burning fossil fuels.

Fast Fact Human activities increase the level of greenhouse gases. Carbon dioxide is released by burning coal, wood, and oil. Methane is given off by rice fields, garbage dumps, and rotting materials.

See Also → • **atmosphere** • **carbon** • **pollution**

Gyroscope

A gyroscope is a heavy wheel that spins on an axle, untouched inside a frame. The spinning wheel spins freely even when the frame is moved.

How Gyroscopes Work

Every spinning object tends to keep spinning on its axis unless something stops it. A spinning object also resists tipping on its axis. When spinning fast, a gyroscope resists being pushed over.

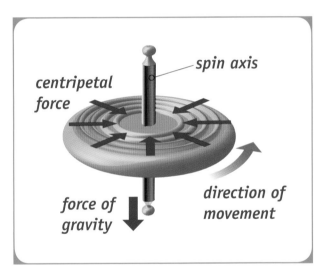

centripetal force

spin axis

force of gravity

direction of movement

A spinning object on Earth will eventually stop due to outside forces, which include gravity.

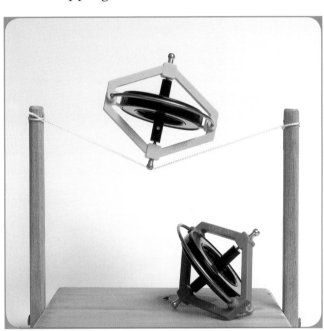

When spinning, a toy gyroscope tends to stand up.

Uses of Gyroscopes

Gyroscopes are used in navigation instruments, such as compasses, to provide information about where ships and airplanes are heading. Movement caused by air turbulence or heavy seas does not affect a gyroscope. Gyroscopes are used to guide torpedoes, missiles, satellites, and spacecraft. They are also used in toys.

Fast Fact Automatic pilot devices, which use gyroscopes, can steer an airplane closer to a course than a human pilot can.

See Also → • center of gravity • gravity • kinetic energy

Habitat

A habitat is the area in which a species of plant or animal lives. Each habitat includes all the living and non-living things in the area.

Types of Habitats

The Earth provides many different types of habitats for living things. Habitats are constantly changing. A tree, a rock, a cave, a cliff face, a small coral within a reef, or a whole coral reef are all habitats.

Wetland habitats support plants and animals that live in and around freshwater.

Changing tide at a seashore provides habitats for species that can live both under water and on land.

Desert habitats support species that can survive on very little water.

Populations in Habitats

A population is a number of the same species that live within a particular habitat. A population grows when there are more births than deaths in that population. Some species can survive in habitats with very different conditions, such as the fox, which can live in wood, desert, or farm habitats. Other species have very specific requirements.

Fast Fact The areas deep inside caves are habitats for many creatures that never see the light of day.

Some habitats can support a large population of one species.

Hardness

Hardness is one of the key physical properties of a substance. It describes how much force a substance can resist.

How Hardness is Measured

Hardness is measured by testing if one substance will scratch another. Harder substances scratch softer ones. Friedrich Mohs (1773–1839) devised a scale against which the hardness of a substance is measured, called the Mohs scale. It arranges ten minerals from 1 to 10. The higher the number, the harder the mineral.

Talc is the softest mineral, and is rated 1 on the Mohs scale.

Diamond is the hardest substance on the Mohs scale, and is rated 10.

A diamond-tipped drill is hard enough to cut other materials with ease.

Fast Fact Graphite is a gray–black carbon mineral used in pencils. A pencil is graded using H for hard and B for bold, or soft.

See Also → • mineral
• physical property

Heart

The heart is part of the circulatory system in animals. It is a ball of muscle that pumps constantly. This constant pumping forces blood around the body through a system of blood vessels.

Structure of the Heart

Different animals have hearts with different structures. The human heart is divided into two sides, left and right. The heart is made of a special type of muscle, called cardiac muscle. The heart muscle itself has a rich supply of blood vessels.

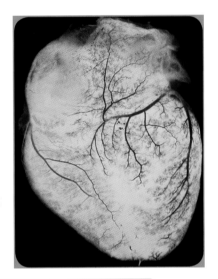

Blood vessels on the outside of the heart supply blood to the heart muscle.

Function of the Heart

The function of the heart is to constantly pump blood around the body. It does this by beating, or contracting. Heart muscle is able to pump constantly without tiring.

The heart is like a double pump. The right side pumps blood to the lungs to pick up oxygen. The oxygen-rich blood then returns to the left side of the heart. From there it is pumped out to the rest of the body.

Fast Fact A healthy adult human heart is about the size of a closed fist.

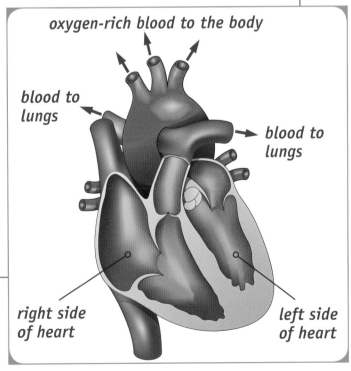

oxygen-rich blood to the body

blood to lungs

blood to lungs

right side of heart

left side of heart

A human heart is divided into left and right sides.

See Also → • blood
• circulatory system

Heat

Heat is a form of energy. It is the energy of the movement of molecules in a substance. The faster the molecules move in a substance, the hotter that substance is.

How Heat Works

Heat energy is the combined energy of all the molecules moving in a substance. When objects are heated, their molecules move faster. When solid objects are heated, they tend to expand because their molecules move further apart.

Heat transfers, or moves, from hot objects to cooler ones. Heat is transferred through substances by:

- conduction – the movement of heat energy through a substance or from one substance to another
- convection – the transfer of heat energy by moving liquids or gases
- radiation – the transfer of heat by rays, called infrared rays

Fast Fact The molecules in cold objects move about very little because they have very little heat energy.

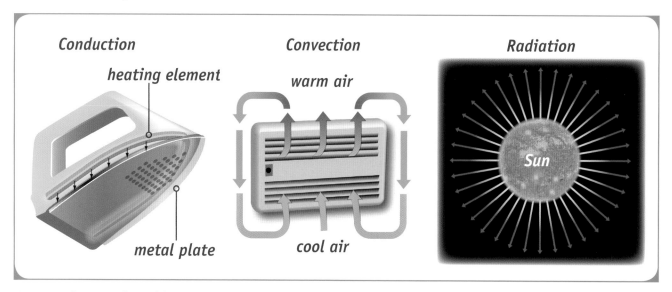

Conduction

heating element

metal plate

Convection

warm air

cool air

Radiation

Sun

Heat can be transferred by conduction, convection, or radiation.

Sources of Heat

Anything that gives off heat is a source of heat. The Sun is the main source of heat on Earth. People also use other heat sources, such as burning wood and coal. Heat is released:

- by nuclear reactions in the Sun
- by volcanoes and geysers from deep inside the Earth
- by chemical reactions that occur when coal, wood, natural gas, or any other fuel burns
- by nuclear reactions in reactors used to generate electricity
- by friction when two objects rub against each other
- when electricity flows through a resistance in a circuit

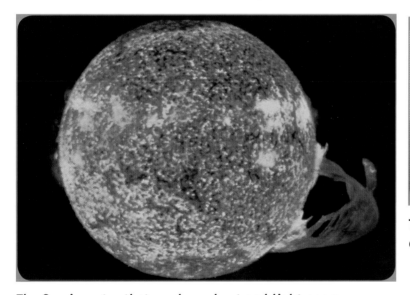

The Sun is the main source of heat on Earth.

The Sun is a star that produces heat and light energy.

How Heat is Sensed

Heat is a form of radiation that we do not see with our eyes but we sense with our skin. Heat is felt through the skin by heat sensors, or receptors, that react to heat. These do not measure the temperature of an object, but judge whether it is hotter or colder than our skin.

See Also → • conductor • convection • energy • radiation • ray • temperature

Human

A human, or a person, is a vertebrate animal. Humans are classified as mammals. Like all mammals, humans have hair and the mother produces milk to feed her offspring. All humans are members of the species *Homo sapiens*.

Structure of the Human Body

The human body is made up of a number of body systems. These systems include the circulatory, skeletal, digestive, and nervous systems. The study of the structures of the human body is called anatomy.

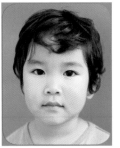

The human species is made up of different races.

Classifying Humans

Kingdom	Animal
Phylum	Chordate
Class	Mammal
Order	Primate
Family	Hominid
Genus	*Homo*
Species	*sapiens*
Scientific Name	*Homo sapiens*
Common Name	Humans, or people

Fast Fact The scientific name for the human species, *Homo sapiens*, means "thinking man."

Australopithecus
3 million years ago

Homo erectus
750,000 years ago

Homo sapiens
100,000 years ago to present

Scientists believe modern humans are the result of a long process of evolution.

30

See Also → • Animal Kingdom • classification • mammal • vertebrate

Hydrogen

chemical symbol **H**

Hydrogen is a colorless, odorless gas. It is the lightest of all the elements. It reacts very readily with many other substances.

Properties of Hydrogen

The properties of hydrogen are:

- it is the lightest element
- it has no taste, smell, or color
- it combines with many other substances to form a variety of compounds, including water

A hydrogen atom has just one proton, which makes up the nucleus, and one electron.

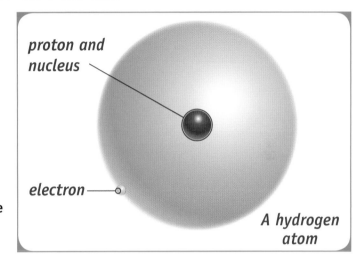

proton and nucleus

electron

A hydrogen atom

Fast Fact Hydrogen was used to inflate early airships, but it proved to be highly explosive and unsafe.

Uses of Hydrogen

Hydrogen is used in many different things. It is combined with nitrogen to make fertilizers and cleaners. When combined with carbon and oxygen it can make artificial fibers. It is also used for refining metal from ores and as fuels for space shuttles.

Liquid hydrogen is used as rocket fuel.

See Also → • element and compound
• gas • physical property
• water

31

Ice Age

An ice age is a cold period when temperatures fall and large sheets of ice, called ice sheets and glaciers, cover much of the Earth's surface.

How Ice Ages Happen

Ice ages happen when, for some reason, less of the Sun's heat is trapped in the Earth's atmosphere. During an ice age, the temperature is much lower than it is today. These temperature changes may have been caused by changes in the tilt of the Earth's axis and its orbit around the Sun.

Ice covered much of the Earth's surface more than 10,000 years ago during the last ice age.

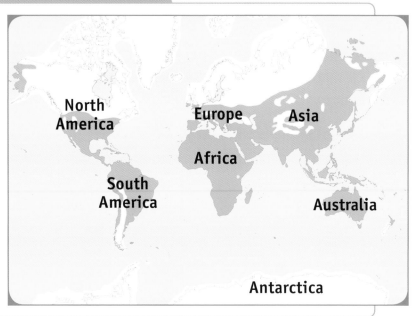

Evidence of Past Ice Ages

Scientific evidence suggests that there have been up to 20 major ice ages in Earth's history. Many rock surfaces show signs of being scoured or smoothed by glaciers. Ice ages occur on Earth about every 150 million years. The last ice age ended about 10,000 years ago.

Fast Fact The term "ice age" was first used in 1837, and originally referred to the ice age of the Pleistocene epoch.

Some of the Ice Ages on Earth		
Geological Time in Which It Began	**Beginning of Ice Age**	**End of Ice Age**
Precambrian eon	650 million years ago	570 million years ago
Ordovician period	440 million years ago	430 million years ago
Carboniferous period	330 million years ago	250 million years ago
Pleistocene epoch	1.64 million years ago	10,000 years ago

See Also → • geological time
• glacier

Iceberg

Ice Age
Iceberg

An iceberg is a large mass of ice that has broken away from a glacier or ice sheet. An iceberg is made of frozen freshwater. Icebergs float and drift in the ocean.

How Icebergs Form

Icebergs form when moving glaciers reach the sea and parts of the glacier break off. An iceberg can also break away from an ice sheet, or a thick mass of ice and snow covering a large area of land or sea.

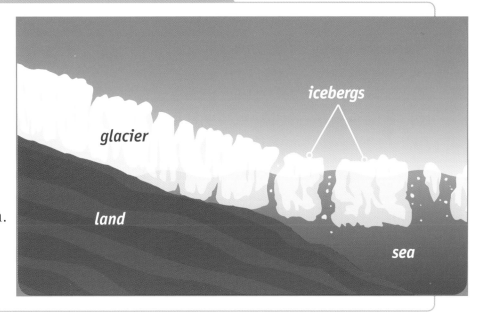

Glaciers break off in the sea and form icebergs.

Where Icebergs are Found

Icebergs today are found in the Arctic and Antarctic regions. Icebergs in the northern seas come from Greenland, and those in the southern seas come from Antarctica. Icebergs are carried through the seas by winds and ocean currents.

Fast Fact Around 90 percent of an iceberg is hidden beneath the surface of the sea.

Icebergs are often found in groups around Antarctica in the Southern Ocean.

See Also → • glacier • ice age
• ocean

33

Incline

An incline is used to make work easier. It is easier to push a heavy load up an incline, or a slope, than it is to lift it straight up.

How Inclines Work

Moving something up an incline uses less energy and makes work easier. Using an incline means the load is moved over a greater distance, but with less effort than would be needed to lift the load straight up. The same amount of work is done overall, but less effort, or force, is used over the greater distance.

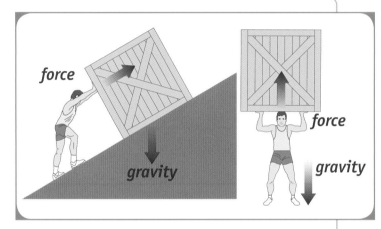

A slope makes it possible to raise heavy loads.

Screws

A screw is a special kind of incline that is wound into a spiral shape. Turning a screw is like pushing something up a spiral ramp. Less effort is needed to wind a screw into something than to drive a nail into it.

Fast Fact Many ancient peoples used inclines to help them build huge stone monuments.

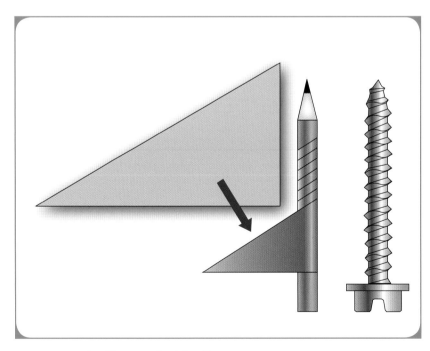

A screw works like a spiral incline.

See Also → • energy • force • gravity • machine

Indicator

Incline
Indicator

An indicator is a substance that changes color in different conditions. Indicators are used to test the acidity or alkalinity of a solution.

Uses of Indicators

Indicators are used when the acidity or alkalinity of substances needs to be tested. The acidity of soil affects plant growth, so a universal indicator is used to test soils and find out if they are acidic, alkaline, or neutral. Different indicators are used to test different parts of the pH range.

LEMON JUICE VINEGAR WATER BAKING SODA DISHWASHER POWDER

RED CABBAGE JUICE INDICATOR

Fast Fact The juices of red cabbages and berries make color solutions that work as indicators.

When substances such as lemon juice and vinegar are added to red cabbage juice, the solution changes color and indicates the pH of the substance.

Indicator Papers

Litmus paper contains a chemical that changes color when its pH, or acidity, changes. It turns red in acidic solutions or blue in alkaline solutions.

Universal indicator paper is made using a mixture of indicator substances. It measures all levels of pH and it uses different colors to indicate different levels.

full range
pH 1-14

A universal indicator measures the full scale of acidity and alkalinity.

See Also → • acid • alkali • lichen
• solution

Inheritance

Inheritance is the passing on of characteristics from parents to their children. Characteristics are passed on through the genes. Family members have similar characteristics because of the common genes they inherit.

How Inheritance Works

Inheritance works through genes, which hold the instructions for an organism's characteristics. Some genes, such as the one that decides eye color, come in various forms, called alleles. A person has two genes for each characteristic, and one is inherited from each parent. When these two genes are different alleles, or forms, one masks the effect of the other. An allele for brown eyes will mask the allele for blue eyes. Brown is said to be dominant and blue is said to be recessive.

eye color

hair type and color

skin tone

height

Some characteristics that are inherited from our parents can be seen easily.

Inheritance and Offspring

Inheritance explains how parents produce offspring like themselves. Offspring look similar to their parents because they inherit a mixture of genes from their parents. All living things, including animals, plants, and microscopic organisms, such as algae, inherit their genetic material.

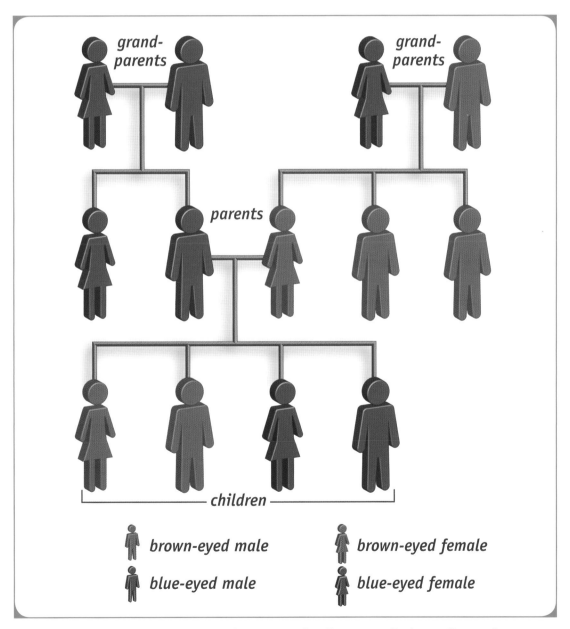

The pattern of inheritance can be shown on a family tree, called a pedigree chart.

See Also → • chromosomes • gene
• reproduction

37

Insect

An insect is an invertebrate animal with six legs. The body of an insect is divided into three parts, called the head, thorax, and abdomen. Most insects have wings.

Structure of Insects

The three sections of the body of an insect are:

- the head, with specialized organs that include eyes, antennas, and mouth parts

- the thorax, to which the legs and wings attach

- the abdomen, which contains the digestive parts and the reproductive organs.

An insect has a head, thorax, and abdomen.

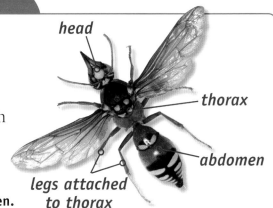

head
thorax
abdomen
legs attached to thorax

Life Cycle of Insects

Insects have different patterns to their life cycles. All insects reproduce by laying eggs. Some young insects look like miniature adults of the species and are called nymphs. Other insects go through great changes called metamorphosis, and the adults do not look at all like the young.

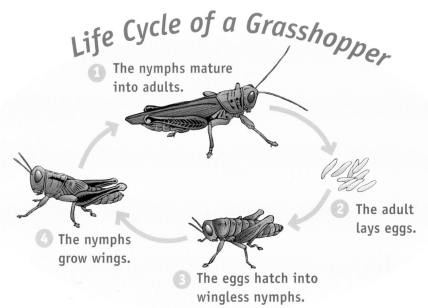

Life Cycle of a Grasshopper

1. The nymphs mature into adults.
2. The adult lays eggs.
3. The eggs hatch into wingless nymphs.
4. The nymphs grow wings.

Classifying Insects

There are a large number of orders, or subgroups, of the Insect Class. Insect orders are grouped according to leg and wing structures.

Classifying Insects

Kingdom	Animal
Phylum	Arthropod
Class	Insect
Number of Orders	29
Number of Families	949
Number of Species	At least 950,000

Some Orders of Insects

Order	Description
Dragonflies	Carnivorous, with two pairs of equal-sized wings
Grasshoppers and crickets	Powerful hind legs for jumping
Butterflies and moths	Scaly bodies and wings
Bugs	Two pairs of wings, with the front wings partly hardened
Beetles	Front wings hardened and used as a wing cover
Flies	Single pair of flight wings
Ants, bees, and wasps	Narrow waist and two pairs of wings hooked together

Fast Fact More than one million species of insects have been identified to date. This is more than any other group of animals.

See Also → • arthropod • classification
• invertebrate
• metamorphosis

Insulator

An insulator is a material that blocks or resists the transfer of energy. An insulator resists or slow downs the movement of electricity, heat, or sound.

How Insulators Work

Insulators work by blocking the transfer of energy. Most materials other than metals are good insulators of electricity. These materials work by blocking or slowing the transfer of energy by electrons. Materials such as wood, plastic, and cloth insulate heat and prevent its transfer. Sound is insulated by materials that prevent soundwaves passing through.

Electrical wires have an insulated coating of plastic.

Fast Fact Nerves in the body conduct electricity and are surrounded by insulating fat.

Uses of Insulators

Most electrical insulators today are plastics. Electrical wires have a plastic coating to stop electricity escaping from them.

Heat insulators such as oven mitts block the transfer of heat from a hot pot to the hand.

Sound insulation, such as thick glass in windows, can block out loud noise, such as traffic.

Insulation in a house prevents heat transfer, and can reduce both heating and cooling costs.

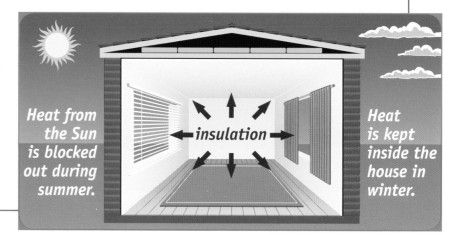

Heat from the Sun is blocked out during summer.

←insulation→

Heat is kept inside the house in winter.

40

See Also → • conductor • electricity • heat

Intestines

Intestines are part of the digestive system in animals. They are a hollow tube that absorbs nutrients and produces waste.

Structure of the Intestines

The human intestine is made up of the small and large intestines. The small intestine sits curled up in the lower abdomen. It comes after the stomach in the digestive system. The large intestine surrounds the small intestine. At the end of the large intestine is the anus, where waste exits the digestive system.

The small intestine is narrower but much longer than the large intestine.

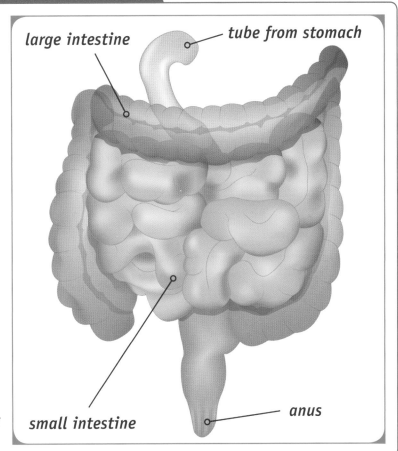

large intestine

tube from stomach

small intestine

anus

Function of the Intestines

The small intestine breaks down food and absorbs nutrients into the body. The large intestine absorbs water from waste before the waste is passed out of the body.

Fast Fact The intestines are also known as the gut or bowels.

See Also → • **digestive system**
• **nutrient**

Invertebrate

An invertebrate is an animal without a backbone. There are many different types of invertebrates. Some invertebrates have no skeleton at all. Others have their skeleton outside their body.

Types of Invertebrate Animals

Invertebrate species can look very different from each other. Sponges, jellyfish, corals, mollusks, worms, arthropods, and starfish are all invertebrates.

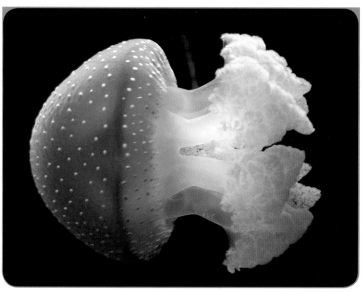

A jellyfish is an example of a soft-bodied invertebrate, which has no skeleton.

Arthropods, such as spiders, are invertebrates with an external skeleton, or hard outer covering.

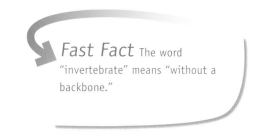

Fast Fact The word "invertebrate" means "without a backbone."

Classifying Invertebrates

Invertebrate animals are grouped according to their body structures.

Fast Fact More than 95 percent of all animals are invertebrates.

Some Phyla of Invertebrates

Phylum		Description
Sponges		Sponges are loose groupings of cells. The cells can move and change functions.
Cnidarians (jellyfish, coral, and relatives)		These invertebrates have a simple body with a single opening.
Segmented worms		Worms are tube-like animals with soft bodies, and a mouth and an anus.
Mollusks		Mollusks have a body with a head, a foot, and a lump that covers the internal organs. They sometimes have a shell.
Arthropods (including insects, spiders, crabs, and crustaceans)		Arthropods have a segmented body and jointed legs.
Echinoderms (including starfish, sea urchins, and sea cucumbers)		These invertebrates have bodies with radiating arms and a spiny outer covering.

See Also → • **Animal Kingdom**
• **arthropod** • **classification**
• **mollusk** • **worm**

Iron

 chemical symbol **Fe**

Iron is a very dense, silver–gray metal. Iron is the fourth most common element found in Earth's crust.

Properties of Iron

The properties of iron are:

- it is soft and easily shaped
- it rusts when exposed to air and moisture, and forms iron oxide
- it is magnetic
- it is very dense, or heavy, for its size
- it easily combines with other metals to form alloys

Where Iron Occurs

Iron occurs in the ground as iron ore. Iron ore is a mixture of iron and other substances. Iron occurs as mineral ores such as hematite.

Iron can be extracted, or separated, from hematite ore in rocks.

Fast Fact Sources of iron in food include meat, egg yolk, wheat germ, and leafy green vegetables.

Rust

Iron reacts with air and water to form iron oxide, which is called rust. When the oxygen in air combines with iron, it forms iron oxide on the surface of the metal. Iron objects need to be protected in some way to prevent rust. Painting iron is one way to protect it from rust.

Rust forms a coating on the outside of iron objects such as screws.

Uses of Iron

Iron is mixed with carbon and other elements to make the alloy steel. Adding carbon to iron makes steel that is harder, stronger, and less easy to shape and stretch than pure iron. Stainless steel is an alloy made by mixing iron, carbon, and nickel or chromium. Stainless steel resists rust.

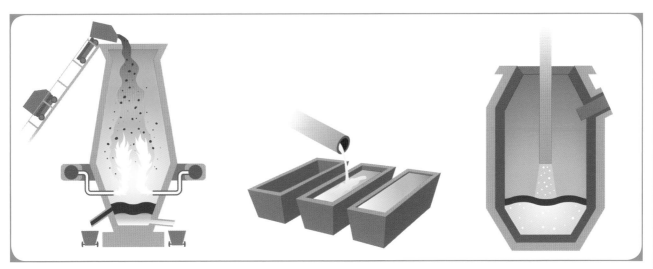

Rocks containing iron are put into a blast furnace with other ingredients.

Pure molten iron is poured off and cooled in molds.

The iron is then heated with carbon to make steel.

See Also → • element and compound
• metal • mineral
• physical property • rusting

Jupiter

Jupiter is the fifth planet from the Sun. Jupiter is a giant planet, and the largest planet in the Solar System. The surface of Jupiter is a made up of swirling gases.

Profile of Jupiter

Diameter at Equator	88,846 miles (142,984 kilometers)
Mass	318 times the mass of Earth
Volume	1400 times the volume of Earth
Average Distance from Sun	483, 675,336 miles (778,400,000 kilometers)
Revolution Around Sun	11.87 Earth years
Number of Moons	At least 63
Rotation on Axis	9.93 hours
Gravity	2.36 times greater than Earth
Cloud-top Temperature	−234 degrees Fahrenheit (−148 degrees Celsius)
Named After	Roman king of the gods

Jupiter is a giant planet made up mostly of gases.

Structure of Jupiter

Jupiter's atmosphere consists of clouds of hydrogen and helium gases. Beneath these clouds is liquid hydrogen. Beneath the liquid hydrogen is hydrogen in the form of a liquid metal. In the center is a hot rocky core.

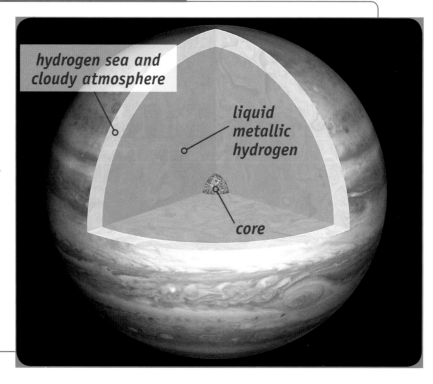

hydrogen sea and cloudy atmosphere

liquid metallic hydrogen

core

Inside Jupiter

Special Features of Jupiter

Some of the special features of the planet Jupiter are:

- Jupiter is much bigger than any other planet in the Solar System.

- The Great Red Spot is a huge hurricane in Jupiter's atmosphere. It has lasted for at least 400 years, and is the size of three Earths.

- A thin system of three rings around Jupiter seems to be made of small rocks and dust particles.

Fast Fact Jupiter is known as a gas giant because it is made up mainly of gases and does not have a solid surface.

The Great Red Spot moves westward around the planet, but it does not move north or south.

Observing Jupiter

1609	1994	1995
Galileo Galilei uses a telescope to view Jupiter's four largest moons: Callisto, Ganymede, Europa, and Io.	Jupiter is hit by the fragments of the Shoemaker-Levy 9 comet.	The *Galileo* space probe first approaches and observes Jupiter and some of its moons.

See Also → • planet • Solar System • Sun

Kinetic Energy

Kinetic energy is the energy of movement. Any moving object has kinetic energy. The study of kinetic energy is called dynamics.

How Kinetic Energy Works

Kinetic energy is the result of motion. The faster an object moves, the more kinetic energy it has. Even an object that appears to be at rest is in motion. The kinetic energy of moving molecules is called heat energy. Temperature is a measure of this energy. In a very cold object, the molecules are moving slowly. In a very hot object, the molecules are moving much faster.

Fast Fact The word "kinetic" comes from the Greek word "kinetikos," meaning "to move."

The faster a skateboard goes, the more kinetic energy it has.

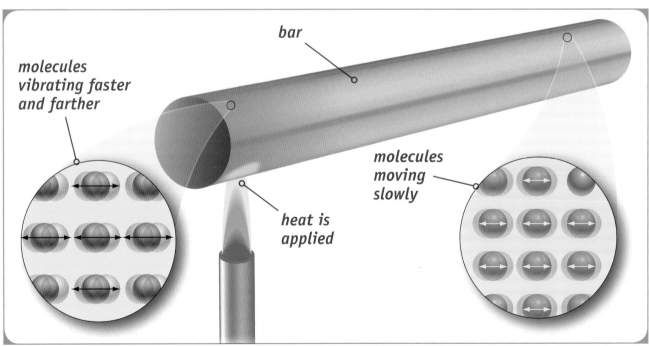

Heating adds energy to the molecules of the bar, making them vibrate faster and farther.

See Also → • energy • force • movement • potential energy